THE

OLD CURRENT

———

THE
OLD CURRENT

POEMS

Brad Leithauser

ALFRED A. KNOPF

NEW YORK

2025

THIS IS A BORZOI BOOK PUBLISHED BY
ALFRED A. KNOPF

Copyright © 2025 by Brad Leithauser

aaknopf.com

Knopf, Borzoi Books, and the colophon are registered trademarks of Penguin Random House LLC.

LIBRARY OF CONGRESS CATALOGING-IN-PUBLICATION DATA
Names: Leithauser, Brad, author.
Title: The old current : poems / Brad Leithauser.
Description: First edition. | New York : Alfred A. Knopf, 2024.
Identifiers: LCCN 2024015136 (print) | LCCN 2024015137 (ebook) |
ISBN 9780593802809 (hardcover) | ISBN 9780593802816 (ebook)
Subjects: LCGFT: Poetry.
Classification: LCC PS3562.E4623 O428 2024 (print) |
LCC PS3562.E4623 (ebook) | DDC 811/.54—dc23/eng/20240404
LC record available at https://lccn.loc.gov/2024015136
LC ebook record available at https://lccn.loc.gov/2024015137

Jacket image: *Kamogawa in Kyoto* (detail) by Hiroshi Yoshida.
Photograph: The Abram C. Joseph and Ruth F. Ring Collection,
gift of Miss Ruth F. Ring / Bridgeman Images
Jacket design by Ariel Harari

Manufactured in Canada
First Edition

For

Rick Lyon
and
John Chapman—

friends
of the
long ago
and the
here and now

CONTENTS

In 1982, when my first book was published, I was living in Japan. One day a hefty airmail box from Knopf arrived at the legal research institute where I was working. There it was: copies of *my book* . . . I was of course tempted to tear the thing open with my bare hands, but a secretary at the institute, sensing a summons to ceremony, asked me to hold off while she went to fetch a "special knife" (which looked a lot like a regular knife). It's a moment I treasure both for itself and for its forecasting of the way a life in poetry would involve both ample waiting and the impulse to transform routine into rite.

A third of a century later, I returned to Japan and the "old current" of my title. A stubborn river of indebtedness followed close behind me, debts I mean partially to repay here. "Return to Japan" is dedicated to Yosuke Ejima and Yuha Kajima; "Lullabies for a Newborn" to Leena Cowart and Teddy Cowart; "Escalation" to Ann Close; "Prism Cell" to Alice Quinn; "Six Quatrains" to Steve O'Donnell; "Philosopher's Walk" to Jonathan Singleton; "Some Stranger's Passport" to Wendy Watson; "The Third Suitor" to Lisa Raskin; "In the English Department Lounge" to David Sofield; "Icarus and His Kid Brother" to Howland Chickering; "A Single Flight" to Eric Sawyer; "Total" to Richard Kenney; "The Old Current" to John Freeman; "A Beach of Big White Stones" to Jamie Bernstein. "Words Turn Back" is dedicated to the memory of Christopher Carduff. "A Young Farewell," to the memory of Lawrence Cowart.

THE

OLD CURRENT

———

LOOK

not in your heart,
that unreliable
narrator, but
   to an earth apart:

   one devoted to creation
as the volcano,
to revision
   as the ocean.

I

DARKER

LULLABIES FOR A NEWBORN

1. *A Night . . .*

What is it now,
You little needling?
Needing a bottle? Or
A bottle's warmth? Or
A rare rocking motion
I've not yet learned
To administer?
Or—simply—company?

Of course it's clear
You're right: the dark
Is big, and unaccountable,
And darkly sinister,
And you upon an ocean
Unable to steer,
Drifting from shore.
Lacking words, still

You must learn faith
In the odd notion
That the day's belongings
Will reappear,
Dark be fended off,
At least for the night,
And the roomy harbor
Once more come to light.

II. . . . *And a Night* . . .

What is it now,
You show-er of lung-power?
Frankly, this isn't how
I hoped to while
The darkest hour
When the streetlights,
Cold as the stars, but bigger,
Hum to each other.

In truth, I was hoping
For a welcomed return
To that peaceable
Kingdom of fern-
Blanketed valleys and
Pillowy hills—an earlier,
Other terrain now known
As the Land Before You Were Born.

Silly—my thinking this way,
Given you so insistent
That, howsoever far the mind may
Span the spilt milk galaxies,
No universe exists
Where you are nonexistent.
On this, you are unanimous.
Always, you were with us.

III.   . . . *And a Night* . . .

What is it now,
Our little jackpot, un-
Likely winner of some
Bizarre scavenger
Hunt whose first leg
Sent an armless swimmer
Tailing off in search
Of a sheltering egg?

You win. I'm up, I'm here.
Up to marvel once more
At your simple knack
(Something the greatest
Artists might envy you for)
Of rendering your circle
Dazed and docile
And subservient.

What is the latest?
You ask for nothing
But a few slugs of milk,
A little warmth—
Nothing but that sea
And moon and stars
You our universal heir
Already claim as yours.

IV. . . . *And Tonight*

What is it now?
What is it now?
You cannot talk
But let's be clear . . .
I wish you would explain
Why it was you called me here.
You don't seem hungry.
Or in pain.

Was it fear?
Perhaps a scientist
Might tell us when
The newborn brain
First learns to fear.
I would convince you,
If I could, that nothing
Shall harm you here.

Or was it love? Some small
But urgent need for touch?
I fear no scientist
Could tell us much
About when love
First primes the soul.
Let's go with that—with love.
You called. I heard your call.

ELEGY FOR AN ART HISTORIAN

(John Varriano, 1943–2016)

Would I write some lines for you? Well—I felt flattered.
You envisioned today's fête, your friends together,
And while you wouldn't be with us, of course,
Wished us this fine weather.

Under dark, ice-skidding skies you left us shattered
At the loss of your warmth and that jumpy, exhilarated
Curiosity of yours, which left both you
And your subjects illuminated.

Time homes forward, and our lives are scattered
In a bright, predictable upheaval
Of daily demands, until, now and then,
Your gaze, voice . . . you're back, John, an act of retrieval

Restoring what for us has always mattered:
Painterly grace, like mountainous white clouds flying
On their high, mysterious errands,
Imponderable and undying.

FORTY-FIVE YEARS ON

All of us thrown
Together, room and dorm, assignees of
Strict, unreadable designs known
To the Housing Office alone,

Our postings based
Not, it seems, on money, looks, faith,
Height, mastery of the standardized test,
Shared esoteric tastes (or even lack of taste)—

And yet, for some,
It was a grounding of sentiments
To compass a wayward lifetime,
Beginning—shyly—"Where are you from?"

*

All of us drawn
Apart, riven by a line, likewise unreadable
And strict, between those who go on
And the ones now gone.

Once again, there's
No pattern, it all has little to do
With what we've done: jobs we chose, hours
We kept, the hopes, the private pleasures.

We'd start anew,
Even now, if we knew how. The old words
Return, slightly out of true
(Though the heart's still true): "Where are you . . ."

WORDS TURN BACK

We had a parting of the ways, some ways back.
　　—Or perhaps more accurate to say
You halted and we kept going. The outcome,
Come what will, is a widening divide, each day

Drawing us precisely one further day apart, each
　　New event—indifferent or passionate,
Blissful, blighted—becoming a little puzzle-piece
We've fitted into our lives and you have not.

The living move on—there is no other way—
　　And yet our words turn back,
And often we most meaningfully speak
Over the shoulder.
　　　　　　　We hike a well-worn track

Of unfixed origin, and if we live
　　Prospectively—no other way—we live for the small
Intermissions as well, when words turn back
Into the substances we'd recall,

Where to utter your name again
　　Is to materialize you
Just as once you were, and to be
Re-reminded, while you vanish anew,

How we brave the same obstacles and come,
　　Seasonably, to the same recognition
Of a reviving uncertainty: our unreckonable
But identical destination.

PHILOSOPHER'S WALK

The year's first snowfall, so you trek alone
Out to the Point—resentful, on the long way back,
    Of the loose footprints on the track,
        Though the prints are your own.

END OF AN ADVENTURER

He's ridden on a carpet on a camel's back,
    In a bathysphere, a glider, a sealskin kayak,
A dhow, a dogsled, and now a gurney,
    Silent and smooth, for the final journey.

A YOUNG FAREWELL

I love you so loud
Was the three-year-old's cry
To her grandfather supine
On his deathbed. Goodbye. Goodbye,

As we humbly consign
All that's material
To the underground,
Just as is called for—save

A stubborn, unbowed
Prayer that the proverbial
Silence of the grave
Forever echo with her sound.

II

ABROAD

THE THIRD SUITOR

A sleeting, steel-gray March day,
And an opening mist discloses
Singular doings on François Premier:

Madame Quesnell, a retired postal
Clerk and stout stanchion of propriety,
Is rifling a trash receptacle—

Yet who could resist such felicity?
Roses, still half-wrapped, and from Lachaume,
The oldest florist in the city . . .

Roses, *roses* in the sleet; red, redolent *roses*—
A boon beyond all fantasy.
Oh, she had to take them home.

On a bus, shy in the wilting daylight
(Not for having prised a treasure horde
From the trash, but for fearing somebody might

Think *she* meant to put one over,
Posing, for the other shivering passengers,
As a lady bearing favors from a lover),

She carried them at her breast, as one does
With a fretful infant, while peering
Through the icy, down-running windows.

In truth, you might have seen her whispering
Reassurances to those roses of hers,
As to a child briefly lost and now restored.

Clear enough, the outlines of the plot:
One guilty party—male. One victim—female.
Outrage; penance; a peace offering. (But the female not

Buying it.) Both young, in all likelihood.
He, a man of means. She, rich in pride—
Which was all to the good.

She—the girl—cries, *You don't deserve my heart,*
And bolts; he will not see her weep.
He in pursuit—*We just need a new start . . .*

She struts along. *You think my love's for sale?*
He follows. *I need you, need you at my side.*
The roses wait behind, enthroned on a trash heap.

No one could have done them better.
In her tiny flat, Mme. Q turned the heat down low
(And put on another sweater).

Stems trimmed. Water changed each day.
Nightly soaks in her footbath bowl.
Petals refreshed with an atomizer spray.

Amazing, how long she husbanded the bloom.
And each time she turned the key
Into her living/dining/sitting room

It was to a glow like a drummer's roll,
Glow of a love-driven gift—as if indeed she
Had received them from some beau.

Oh, not the suitor who, once, might've come
To tug her arm through some public park,
Lunging, garrulous, half-handsome

(A hand on her waist to make the heart quicken),
While steering her to the larger trees
(Where the flattened shadows thicken);

Nor that figure, slender, punctilious,
Old-fashioned yet never fully out of style,
Who arrives in the end for each of us,

Boots brilliant, hair still mostly dark—
Handsome, too, despite the trace
Of impatience in his thin-lipped smile.

Rather, that suitor she has known
All her life, who *is* life—one's modest destiny—
And who (though latterly grown

A little lax perhaps, like an old, benign
Neighbor nodding half-insensible
Over lunch and a second glass of wine)

Will, some unlikely day, duly recalled to order,
Astound her, astound everyone when
He shambles forward to reward her

With a gift simple yet prodigal,
Reminding her that in his eyes she
Is what she's always been:

A creature rare and indispensable.

A RETURN TO TOKYO

Well past midnight, in an imperial moat
Not so far from Ginza,
A lighter shape, a novel note . . .

Duck after duck having paddled darkly past,
Narrowly riffling the neon-skinned
Ebony depths, now arrives, at last,

This elegant other, this wan one
Of elevated neck and broader wake, that we
Might see the city's visual din redone

Utterly, by a creature ferrying
Full cargoes of scintillant swank
Under each folded wing.

HOW IT LOOKS FROM HERE

(Ilulissat, Greenland)

Crisp off the glacier's mouth
And into the blue water—

Here's a docile, sheeplike herd
A north wind duly shepherds toward

That great squealing slaughter-
house the South.

RETURN TO JAPAN

KANAZAWA

Dusk, clear skies, and rain
Ringing and ringing the pond—
No, water striders—

While the snowy hills
Turn pink before turning white
Once more in the dark.

TOKYO, 5 A.M.

Stripped moon, hung over
Ginza, and a drowsing sun,
Needled by neon;

Stars in a which-ways
Of wholesale abandonment—
Half-lit, halfhearted.

KYOTO

On a steep mountain
Path, too narrow for two, you
Meet your younger self.

A BEACH OF BIG WHITE STONES

Pitted, rutted, ruinous,
Riven, slimed, seaweed slung—
But moons all the same, moons nonetheless.

Forbidding zigzag jags of shore,
Foul and fetid and precarious,
But moons nonetheless, moons all the more.

For you who flew so far a way
To reach this place nobody's seen before
(Or no one else but you today),

Here's your beach of big white moons, a big sea,
Half-blue, half-gray,
And a bled-out sky, pale and watery.

Your skies, renewed. And falling, times without
Number—depositing just such tide-tossed
Moons as will be tumbled about

When tonight's moon, pared to a sliver,
Buries all such sublunary moons
In a wash of black and silver.

THE OLD CURRENT

A gritty bench, a grubby river,
And an ongoing wave of wonderment:
How capable and amazing
Everything is, such people are,

Routinely erecting their
Rare dwellings here, with blazing
Blue pantiled roofs, fitted under a hot
And hazy ring of hills.

. . . So firmly rooted, yet so
Remote from me and a narrow,
Open-plotted upbringing
On a tucked away

Plain in southeast Michigan,
Even as, right here, they
Fashioned their unfigured lives,
Equally at home, equally tucked away.

I'm twenty-seven, maybe too old to be
Upended by this, the manifold
Foreignness of it all, the fulfilling
Glazed grandeur of it all,

But we each come into ourselves
As each can, in our own
Unmetered time (our own sweet way),
And for me this day's more thrilling

Than, even now, I can express:
A Michigan boy, plunked down
In *Japan*—Kyoto, no less—
In the sun, on a bench, by a river.

To my adopted bench I've brought
A lunch all but miraculous
Even if bought
In a minimart much like

Any such shop back home.
Outfitted with free chopsticks
I can't manipulate,
My first lunch in Japan consists

Of utterly raw fish,
And a minnowy plastic fish
Whose mouth squirts soy sauce,
And a translucent slice

Of pickled ginger, and a bed of rice,
Still cool (though my hands are sweaty),
Festooned with airy strips
Of dried seaweed,
                    like confetti,

And nearly forty years later
An exhausted plate of maguro
And unagi in a dive near Penn Station
Reawakes the past, the repast . . .

The seaweed is what does it.
The color does it (wine-dark,
The very hue wine would take
If wine were green),

Or the texture (dry but slippery),
Or its pungent distant scent
(Sun-blasted tidal flats,
Evaporated seas).

I'm sixty-six, and could anything
Reliably be more heartening
Than stray hints that life's brightest events
Are, however far-flung, strung

Along a long old current? Than the presentiment
Of some vast, unglimpsed waterway
Where past and present
Dissolve in an enduring flux?

Dexterous chopsticks lift a block of maki
To my nose, as a here-and-now fades
And I'm closer than in decades
To our young man by the Kamo River.

It was a day in August. It was hot,
And I'd come to an ancient city
To contemplate a sun-splashed river
And an embaying ring of hills.

There are moments, slippery
And salvific, rare and pure
And paradoxical as *old current,*
When the wine turns green.

There are these moments,
A verdant vintage goes
To your head, unclouding a passage
Beyond this one on

A river that, having carried
Cargoes past human reckoning, invites
A further passenger. The lights
Shall be borne. And you be ferried.

III

LIGHTER

ESCALATION

("Man Stabbed to Death in Russia for Saying
Poetry Is Not Real Literature: Cops" —Huffington Post *headline)*

. . . But it gets worse.
In Chino, Chile, a husband-and-wife team
of humanists was gunned down in a "crime of rage,"
say cops, after claiming that blank verse
lacks the potential for
innovation in the modern age.

In Toujours-cum-Fez, Algeria,
eight students were fatally poisoned
(twenty others "plenty sick,"
cops say) in a college cafeteria
after refusing to declare their
allegiance to the limerick.

In Vikingurskyr, Iceland, all
thirty-nine members of a sheep
farmers' collective were incinerated
(a "Saga-style razing": cops) in their meeting hall
after approving a position paper
that called the use of rhyme "outdated."

In an assisted-living facility
in Amherst, MA, a lone marksman
(cops aver: "This guy was no amateur")
slew sixty elderly residents who
had earlier denied the viability
of iambic hexameter.

SIX QUATRAINS

I. AN OGDEN OBSERVATION

Guys will be boys; you can't expect even grown men'll seize
    On those elaborate social niceties
So nicely drawn they're all but subliminal.
      But the women'll.

II. ANONYMOUS'S LAMENT

Though love (it's been said) is a perilous game,
    At times I might wish to be bolder—
Just once to be either the moth or the flame
      And not the candle holder.

III. PARALLEL LIFELINES

Not quite goodbye—you'd have us meet
    Where *this* line, if it never ended,
And this so *near,* likewise extended,
      Conjoin. And wouldn't that be sweet.

IV. WHAT TO BELIEVE: A BIBLICAL EXEGESIS

The garden of Eden?
    Maybe a fable.
Yet you can be certain
      Cain slew Abel.

V. THE PRACTICAL MAN

. . . not only slays the dragon
    But cuts it up, salts it down,
And carts the meat to town
    To sell from the back of his wagon.

VI. LUNAR OBSERVATION

Were stars to drop from their vast vault
    Upon your tongue, you'd feel the bite.
There's nothing sweet about the night.
    Never confuse sugar and salt.

ICARUS AND   HIS KID BROTHER

I.

He yearned to soar.
(His name was Icarus.)

                                    Hell, just one more.
                                    (His nights were liquorous.)

The air was hot.
And his wax soon melted.

                                    Sure, "one last shot,"
                                    which of course he belted,

It was no *myth*
to him who fanned

                                    and chased it with
                                    another and

the air and found
it wouldn't support him.

                                    another round . . .
                                    The brief postmortem

In his defense,
you could say his fall

                                    made no reference
                                    to alcohol,

was no calamity—
until the landing.

                                    to protect his family
                                    and social standing.

II.

From childhood on, the elder's eye
Was hunger-fixed upon the sky;
He was determined man should fly.

The other took things somewhat slower,
And set the bar a little lower
(Set *in* a bar—the partygoer).

One soared and fell. One fell and fell,
As if into a well. Oh well . . .
Yet at the finish—strange to tell—

Their branching pathways left no trace;
Each wore—the noble and the base—
The same stunned wonder on his face.

Each left the earth without a sound.
Each searched for truth until he found
A sea of sorrow. Where he drowned.

IN THE ENGLISH DEPARTMENT LOUNGE

He:

Had we but world enough and time,
This coitus, lady, were no crime;
While not what I would call first-rate,
It seems predestined to be great . . .
I mean, I can do better—much.
I'm out of touch, perhaps, with touch . . .
I would devote a dozen years
To learning how to stroke your ears,
Ten dozen would not be amiss
For mastering the simple kiss,
And so on up the downward chart
Of each clandestine body part,
Had we but time . . . You get me, Ms.:
Time's wingèd things are flying—viz.,
I'm wondering whether it's too late
To ask now for a second date.

She:

How would I leave you? Let me count the ways . . .
I'd leave you at a wintry bus stop, one
Minute after the night's last bus has run.
I'd leave you in the lurch. Or in a daze.
I'd leave you sleeping deeply by the pool,
Sun now ablaze, your skin starting to glow.
I'd leave you on a dime. I'd leave you no
Recourse or peace. I'd leave you for a fool.
Leave you bluffing at cards, and no one folding.

I'd leave you in the dust. I'd leave you holding
The bag—*my* bag—of pot as we stepped through
Airport security. And I'd leave you
To ask, "What in hell did she *mean* by that?"
I'd leave you with the check. I'd leave you flat.

THE MUSES

Sober, we savor
    The drudgingly slow
  Pursuit of a dry-as-dust mystery,
Choosing for Muse stern Clio, who's
  The headmistress of History.

Later, when History's
    History, though,
  And life turns lickerish and liquory,
All night we'd cancan, if we could,
  With some lissome-limbed Terpsichore.

FOR SHEILA, TURNING SIXTY-FIVE

We two too have come
To take for granted such days
   As frequently close

   With lunar rainbows
Beribboning the dusk-dim
   Windowpanes of home.

   If we've done little
To merit so bountiful
   A boon, isn't this

   Typically true
Of all those who happen to
   Light on happiness?

KISSES AFTER NOVOCAINE

Though the half of my tongue
that has sensation
is mostly enjoying this,
it would be gross
exaggeration
to call it bliss—

curious, rather,
to discover I've met
new borders but can't say where,
the soul wholehearted
as ever, and yet
the body not all there.

IV

AT HOME

PERMEABLE WORLDS

I. CLEANSING

You clean your glasses but
Neglect to dry them and you
Put them on and it's all exactly what

You've sidelong suspected:
In the sunlight, round you, floats another
System, of globes, large and small, connected

By flashes off their otherwise
Transparent bodies. Buoyant, upbeat, they go
About their daily enterprise

Of closely monitoring all you do—
In bright, polished, dumbshow
Consultations with each other.

II. TWILIGHT ANESTHESIA

Post-op, though not allowed to drive, you
Remain free to leave. You recall being told,
You won't remember this, but you do—

Vaguishly. And recall—long ago—strange Mr. Skeat—
The block's sole hermit—door barred for years—
Yet stopping Mom, one day on the street,

To rage at how somebody'd rearranged
His sock drawer: yes, he was prepared to swear.
Then he moved away. For everything's changed,

Once they get in: yours is no longer yours.
For all their cunning, and care, the dirty, bold,
Invisible prints are everywhere.

III. A FORAY FEEL

A dusk dive. Down where, fifty feet down,
Colors dependably thin, pigments are vanishing
Altogether. Blue to gray, or gray-brown,

While blackness drops upon the ocean's
Frenzied reef-dwellers, for whom night's ever a surprise.
. . . No matter how gentle you'd make your motions,

You with a handheld spotlight and bubbling tank of air
Don't belong. That's clear as day when, underneath
A narrow coral overhang, your probings bare

A burly moray eel, illumining
Row on row of backward-bent teeth,
And yellow, spite-lit eyes.

SOME STRANGER'S PASSPORT

"Or buying *this*?"
                          The utter absurdity . . .
A long-expired passport? Both had to laugh
At the tag-sale rubbish somebody

Hoped somebody'd pay good money for:
Dented pans, bent spoons, dead bonsai,
Widowed glove, whittled broom, rusty file drawer,

Mismatched anklets, three gnawed dog collars . . .
Yet it turned out the joke was on *her,*
Coughing up a couple of dollars

For the passport, its black-and-white photograph
Having elicited an acute little cry:
"Oh my God! It's Uncle Whittaker!"

It wasn't, of course, and yet
A resemblance arrestingly fine:
Same wide, calm, catlike eyes, wet-

Licked lips (tense with a loosening grin),
Same simple, ample, uplifted
Pompadour, strong fleshy nose, weak fleshy chin . . .

The joke here—another joke—
Was how Whittaker *never* would have carried
A passport; he rarely left Royal Oak.

Detroit-born, Whit in the sixties firmly drifted
Some two miles across the city line,
Never to budge again. (And never married.)

He made a reluctant guest in any home,
Even if (his eyesight compromised
In later years) you volunteered to drive him;

But he'd bend over backward to please
Visitors to his dim, low-ceilinged bungalow.
Self-taught, a pastry chef, Whit favored shiny displays

Of sugary sumptuosity: one, two, even three
Kinds of cake . . . He kept a slew of cats,
Seemingly all of one somnolent ancestry:

Plump, complaisantly heaped, patiently slow,
Less like living creatures than outsized,
Heated welcome mats.

. . . Worlds away wheeled one Mitchell J. Mayfair,
Unlikely doppelgänger, who hurled
Life-ward with a helter-skelter penchant for

The wild and woolly: Iceland, Rhodesia,
Morocco, India, Tibet,
The island of Pohnpei (Micronesia),

Guam, New Guinea, Mauritius—
And Italy, over and over again.
It couldn't all be business—too various.

No, Mayfair, another son of Michigan
(Flint, '24), was your true vagabond, bit
By a boyish, lifelong hunger to "see the world."

Or so conjectured the old passport's new
Owner, Whit's niece, the fantasy-
Spinning Anna-Lisa, who was, at thirty-two,

Working on a novel (subject: Prejudice and Hate),
But in her spare time (the manuscript
Was somewhat stalled) liked to fabricate,

For her dentist fiancé, tales of the debonair
But rugged Mr. Mayfair: a picaresque
Of intrigues, rogueries, and one crushing love affair,

Events scored to the cryptic, heavily
Stamped pages of the passport clipped
To the bulletin board above her writing desk.

In her fiancé's favorite episode
An aging Mayfair, in town for a funeral,
Met with an obstacle on Life's Road:

Whit's car. Ka-boom: a ripped open knee,
And Mayfair going nowhere for a while,
And blameless Whit springing an amazingly

Kind offer: the injured man should convalesce
In Whit's own home. Canny Mitchell J.,
Both laid up and hard up, mulled—and said yes.

(If at this juncture he was all
But broke, Mayfair was somebody who knew well
How to make things break his way.)

So, nights, the two gents would ruminate
Over Heartland-style *patisserie,*
Now and then adjusting, for warmth or weight,

Some dozing and ductile cat,
Their chat companionably
Flowing, forever homing in on that

Incomparable boon, a Motor City boyhood.
Some hard times—both would agree—
But no question life was good,

Good in that metropolis of destiny:
The nation's Arsenal of Democracy,
Later its Engine of Prosperity.

Each was 4-F, tending the War from home:
Bond rallies, banners, all-night factories,
The Motor City revving to a steady roaring hum,

War in the Old World and war
In feverish island-chains nobody could
Have located on a map before.

Global war, everywhere war,
And our own Detroit the fountainhead
Of a rich red molten river on whose far shore

Waited an earth burned free of enemies,
Tyranny yielding to brotherhood
And fealty to the imperishable dead.

Peace was blue and yellow; it was sunshine,
Carting old goods to the junk heap,
New clothes on the clothesline.

Peace was broad river breezes born
Flag-like to flutter, bank to bank, America to
Canada: lands of the free. Was popcorn,

And popped corks; money in the bank;
Sweeter streets, a loiter-and-linger;
It was reborn ornament, chrome and silk and swank.

Was make-up. And nylons. It was barbecue.
And songs more hopeful because no longer
Needing to dwell on hope.

And everyone, everywhere, needing everything:
Cars, stoves, rugs; tools, toys; toasters, lamps, chairs.
Time for a universal refurbishing;

Time for Fill the tank, and Run a hot bath;
Time for This man Likes the Looks of Luxury,
And, Can't decide—why not take both?

Time for Wealth without parallel,
Assembled goods borne on waves so great
All shall be lifted on their swell,

Haves and have-nots in an equality
Banishing those old bugbears,
Prejudice and Hate.

So, nights, talk circles round
To Mitchell's Roman *signora*—a mystery
Woman, bright and dark, simple and profound.

Livia. Livia, a painting come to life:
Hot hazel eyes, and auburn hair.
A quick, unexpected, golden laugh.

Livia was glamorous. Well-educated.
Livia could draw, act, sing.
And she was married, though long separated,

To a detestable s.o.b.,
Who regularly had beaten her,
Though she was a fragile, bird-boned thing.

Livia, daughter of Catholic Italy.
No considering divorce. Or ever leaving
A city that jailed her in misery.

Livia wrote poems. She was so artistic.
And moody, judgmental, severe.
He'd never known anyone so *fatalistic*.

Nothing can change! Ever! And nothing to do
But make dinner, or make love, criticize
Or weep or brood, proud at least in knowing you

Aren't one of the ones deceiving
Themselves, refusing to recognize
That life grows grimmer, year by year.

His *inamorata* had mastered the art
Of holding him intact
While holding him apart,

Knowing perfectly well
He was bewitched and would never, for all he
Chose to struggle, break the spell.

"Hell. I'd resent her, she weren't so pitiful."
    And Whit, munching a cocoa bourbon ball,
Mishearing the last word as *beautiful,*

Smiled sweetly, understandingly,
Just as if he had in fact
Heard and understood it all.

A front porch, a solemn reckoning. Two men,
Such warmth: a brief adieu.
(Fate won't throw them together again.)

One says, "I've learned . . ." and drops the rest.
One nods agreement, looking worn. (Travel is aging,
And some things better unexpressed.)

Then off, on his suave cane—but not before
Once more turning to address the other,
Already sliding behind the heavy door.

The lone world wayfarer, ever engaging,
Has the last word, then. To his all-but-brother
He calls, over his shoulder, "You know, I envy you."

FURRY

"Happy and furry?" she inquires,
                                    of the TV—
but I've tuned out. Uh-oh, this one may be
tough to unriddle. When you're eighty-three,

as she is, with creeping dementia—all
sorts of conundrums rattle by,
and everything the more imponderable

if other faculties are failing too . . .
like hearing, perhaps. A few seconds later,
though, we enjoy a breakthrough,

as our breezy, blow-dried commentator
re-airs his catchphrase, which I move to clarify
by relaying it slowly:
                        "Happy. And. Free."

. . . At day's end, even so, I might prefer
happy and furry, as though she
might yet retrieve days when all of us were

that peculiar entity, a big family—
father, mother, four boys of various
ages and stages—become, like any true family,

denizens of a lair,
wound and bound in a low common smell
(our own must of sweat and hair),

that familial furriness that cordons off a small
walled area while informing a potentially
invasive world, *This is us.*

Happy and furry. The woman's five years dead,
yet just last week the phrase returned
as I, watching a YouTube clip, was shepherded

to an obscure nature site by a tag that posed
a teasing test: TRY NOT TO CRY AS MAMA CHIMP
MOURNS BABY. The test? Frankly, I'm not sure I passed.

Embarrassed, as if being watched, I felt
my eyes prickle as the blinking simian—so loving,
so darkly puzzled—stroked and stroked the silky pelt

of a torso strangely limp
whose russet fire still burned,
though warming neither the dead nor the living.

. . . Furry, then, if not free. We mishear,
misread, we go on misspeaking,
and if our errors pain us, soon they disappear

into an unseen, unseeable, ever-amassing crowd.
Click here. Click. Now. Always, the furious din out there,
and what do our answers count, everything so loud

and larger always than yesterday? We learn to chart
our growth by the billion-, trillion-fold:
Vaster, faster numbers. See me. Click. Give me your heart,

click. *Like* me. . . . So many voices, all seeking,
as I suppose both mothers were, the warm, the old,
the furred primordial lair.

A SINGLE FLIGHT

Here's a memory I can date:
We're still in the old house, and this must be
1961, and I'm eight,

Sitting on the front porch steps, alone.
Dusk. Dad has just now left.
In for a drink, maybe. Or the phone.

Overhead, aglow, a whispering jet:
An object gold and pink, catching a sun
That's just now set.

Then—things come strangely undone.
So *strange*: a crowd above me (high, aloft)
Basking in a sun I cannot see.

How many times that year did I see
A plane plying the blue?
Dozens, surely; hundreds, probably;

And every single one retreated
But this one . . . A sweet summer day unraveling
In Detroit, and I'm, age eight, seated

On the front porch steps, alone,
A yet-starless sky drifting blue to gray,
And I who've never flown

Somehow am airborne, borne anew.
What did the boy do today?
Not much—yet the imagination took wing.

Memory's vagrancies, vacancies . . .
A hundred planes alit in a roofless dome
Alike roaring, fading by degrees,

One by one, till one's left. Which still flies.
Those others? Folded into a sea
Of receding obscurities, capsized skies

From which all color drains,
Gray to near-black; black. Then the cold
Comes down, and but little remains

But the concrete porch steps of home,
And a single aircraft, enchantingly
Illuminated: pink, gold.

The boy loves boys' books, books about
Those glorious explorers
(Cortez, Pizarro) who ventured out

In tiny ships for lands and seas
Bigger than anything anyone foresaw.
(Our world was one of their discoveries.)

And if his books hint at things just a bit unjust—
Cruel, maybe—in their race to colonize,
Years must pass for the boy to digest

Implications of the law
Of lance and cutlass and club, the horrors
At the dark heart of the enterprise.

Some voyages are poisoned from the start,
Wheresoever bound—lacking,
Like the conquistadors, purity of heart—

And nothing good can ensue.
   . . . Not so my airship, whose pink-gold wings
Shimmer, triumphantly, through

A clear and cloudy realm above our own.
In time, the plane will stand for
The joy of any journey into the unknown,

The rising impulse that declares, While things
Here may be fine, still we must go looking
For havens yet more fair.

In heaven's name where were they off to?
Cleveland? Milwaukee? Faraway
Washington? I've often wondered who

Was aboard that night . . . Salesmen, each with a case
Of samples? A retired schoolteacher, playing
Hooky at last? A plumber; a piano tuner; a brace

Of grousing lawyers; a young soldier;
A reformed ex-con; a calmed child sleeping
On Grandpa's bursitic shoulder;

A pair of wimpled nuns, praying;
A lover, reviewing a frayed billet-doux; a dove-gray-
Faced mourner, openly weeping?

Flying stories! Tales, details, endlessly
Spinning out, the flight but a chapter in an arcane,
Colossal novel destined never to see

Completion . . . Strangers, bound only in the one
Instance, a closed chamber of clouded gold,
Parting forever before day's done,

Yet their lives will braid, and rebraid,
Like some multiveined, vast
River threading an emerald delta splayed

Open like a fan—a prospect to behold
(Lucidity come for you at last)
From the round window of a plane.

Porch steps, sunset; a warm, gathering gloom.
Behind me, five lives: two parents plus the three
Brothers with whom I share my room.

Four boys, and all great ones for
Citing injustices, the way-too-many
Ways the other three are favored—so *unfair*.

Justice, sentencing . . . Most novels never get done,
And most lives are lost, yet the six of us go
On writing, without writing down,

The doings of one large family
In one small house—a chronicle richer than any
Book the boy I am will ever come to know.

The earth turns, equally overturns
Empires and families,
While a tiny aircraft burns

All but eternally,
Though once a cast-off spark;
The vagaries of memory

Compose a zigzag flight
Over the storehouse of our being
On whose concrete steps, under a light-

Show of etherealities,
We're left to puzzle how we go on seeing
As the world grows dark.

V

DARKER

PRISM CELL

Sun on the drenched rhododendron
After a blackened hour
Of rain, and see how each
Droplet's prism cell
Is a bright, tiny breach
In a dark walled tower;

See lone multitudes of souls
Waving toward you—at you—
The signal rag of their painfully
Stripped-down plaint of misery
And neglect: hear a plea,
Even now, for a blazing rescue.

MOTEL

To this motel whose neon sign repeats
    NO PETS   NO PETS
Somebody's brought a dog. And then gone out,
   leaving the hound behind.
  It's snowing hard, and nearly three . . .
  Where on earth could her owner be?

So she's begun to bark. Her short, sharp cries
    slowly increase
in bitterness if not in pace and volume.
   She's pumped to go all night,
  clearly—prepared to take her time
  in setting out Her Master's Crime.

Sleepless, I see him nursing one last drink . . .
    He'll drive back drunk,
the old scofflaw—assuming he's not now
    scouring the streets for drugs,
  or cruising round in hot pursuit
  of some shivering prostitute.

BARK BARK BARK BARK . . . I'd like to think that her
    objection here
is that the universe has leashed her to
   a partner so unworthy—
not that the good-for-nothing lout
  whom she belongs to has gone out.

PET PARROT

Wouldn't you know it? Today, too,
    won't do.
In the sparse light of dawn he stands
in low relief at his down-to-earth post
    (a crusted inch of dowel clasped
      In gray and crusty hands)

and vents his fury at the way
    each day
keeps turning out . . . His first cry shatters
the night's drawn stillness, then it's cry on cry,
    a steady, uproared *rrrip, rrrip, rrrip,*
      that leaves the air in tatters.

He has no programs to propose,
    and knows
only that most projects begin
badly and go downhill. But he'll make clear,
    whatever fool we take him for,
      he won't be taken in.

How cankered with injustices
    life is!
The world is worse than deeply flawed
and so much darker than you realize.
    The very air's corrupt with lies.
      The daylight is a fraud.

SCRAP

Adoze on a tar-melting afternoon,
hunched in the lumpy and begrimed clutter
of an old-fashioned service
station's waiting room,

beneath the knocking clatter
of a rotating fan whose painful stuttering
might well be cured
with one spare squirt of oil,

you hear, more distant yet, the whirred whine
of a power tool taking off or putting on
lug nuts on the tires of an
eerily airborne minivan

and the sound has the sound
of food ripped, gulleted, the raw break and bite
of an awakened appetite:
piecemetal meal

for that top-heavy colossus
waiting, within every junkyard's scrapheap,
for the summons out of sleep—
aware and erect and locomotoring at last.

BLAZE

The all but all-
Consuming fire
Of '31
That brought half
The village down,
Ripping from
Its hillside perch
The lean white steeple
Of the state's
Third-oldest church,
Has—2017—
Dwindled to a few unsteady

Embers in the mind
Of a bright schoolboy,
Austin Sills,
Now ninety-four,
Who, pressed for details,
Sometimes supplies
Them garrulously,
With urgent certainty—
Sometimes, querulously,
Wonders when supper will be
Served or whether he
Has eaten it already.

OFF THE CLIFF BY SINGLE STEPS

For *Brisk walks,* read *Brick walls.*
For *Brightening stars,* read *Frightening stare.*
And for *Light soufflé,* read *Tight scuffle.*
For *We shared—Be scared.*

For *She wanted joy,* read *The wasted boy.*
For *Acting grand,* read *Aching gland.*
For *Sweet faces pass?—Sweat, feces, piss.*
Avid uninhibited hands?—Arid uninhabited lands.

For *Whispering lovers* it's *Whimpering losers.*
For *Go along,* it's *So alone.*
For *Lovely sights,* it's *Lonely nights.*
Dreaming she may come?—Dreading the way home.

HAPPY HOUR

The very low-profile party of carpenter ants
    that long ago booked passage on
        a cedar log so immense
    it might have been nicknamed *The Titanic*
are just now seeking to clarify
        (no reason yet to panic,

here while the Happy Hour crowd is forming
    by the hearth in the ski resort's Singing Swan
        and stranger is shyly warming
    to stranger, and, *pop!,* the bartender pours
the night's first prosecco) where the exits might lie,
        as the engine room roars.

TOTAL

For now, this once, a blackened noon.
    Cold silence drops on everything.
. . . It's clear the world is ending soon
    And why in their dead reckoning—
Their voices echoed off the moon—
    The crickets have begun to sing.

ACKNOWLEDGMENTS

———

Two of "Six Quatrains" appeared in *Poetry*; "Look," "Blaze," and four of "Six Quatrains" in *Napkin Poetry Review*; "Icarus and His Kid Brother," "Some Stranger's Passport," and "A Single Flight" in *Literary Matters*; "Furry" in the print edition of *The Common* and "Words Turn Back," "Return to Japan," and "The Old Current" in its online edition.

"Prism Cell" appeared in *Together in a Sudden Strangeness,* an anthology, edited by Alice Quinn, of responses to the Covid pandemic.

Brad Leithauser is the author of eighteen previous books, the most recent of which is *Rhyme's Rooms: The Architecture of Poetry*. He is a former theater critic for *Time,* and the recipient of numerous awards and honors, including a MacArthur Fellowship and a Guggenheim Fellowship. In 2005, he was inducted into the Order of the Falcon by the president of Iceland. A former professor in the Writing Seminars at Johns Hopkins University, he lives in Amherst, Massachusetts.

A NOTE ON THE TYPE

The text of this book was set in Bembo, a facsimile of a typeface cut by Francesco Griffo for Aldus Manutius, the celebrated Venetian printer, in 1495. The face was named for Pietro Cardinal Bembo, the author of the small treatise entitled *De Aetna* in which it first appeared. Through the research of Stanley Morison, it is now generally acknowledged that all old-style type designs up to the time of William Caslon can be traced to the Bembo cut. The present-day version of Bembo was introduced by the Monotype Corporation of London in 1929. Sturdy, well-balanced, and finely proportioned, Bembo is a face of rare beauty and great legibility in all of its sizes.

Composed by North Market Street Graphics
Lancaster, Pennsylvania

Printed and bound by Friesens
Altona, Manitoba

Book design by Pei Loi Koay